ONE HEART TO ANOTHER

ONE HEART TO ANOTHER

ANNETTE WHITAKER

Contents

Words of Wisdom

Commit to the LORD whatever you do, and your plans will succeed.

Proverbs 16:3

In his heart, a man plans his course, but the LORD determines his steps.

Proverbs 16:9

Special Thanks

To Alesa Rivers who inspired and helped me to understand what a blessing my writing would be to others. Her persistence and creative ideas helped make this dream a reality of which I am forever grateful.

A Word From The Author

A leader of integrity teaches followers to be positive, confident, and successful. No other experience in life is as fulfilling as helping others in need. Sharing these experiences in this book of poetry is intended to help others persevere through the joys, the struggles, the hopes, the dreams, the sadness, the laughter, the accomplishments, and the encouragement while persevering through life's journey. May the readers be filled with insight to carry on and the blessings of our Lord and Savior, Jesus Christ.

Memories of the Heart

In Loving Memory of My Grandson
(DeShaun LaTrell Dorsey)

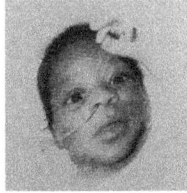

From the very start
Love resides within the heart
Our deepest thoughts lie within
And this is where our Lord begins

God, who sees the heart
Love, he placed there from the start
Cause the heart, He knew, would do its part

So, when this life is at its end
Remember, the heart is where it begins
Warmth, love, peace, comfort, laughter, and tears
The very things that helped you through
Life struggles and life fears

The heart is with you every day
Here, love, we gently tucked away
It will never, ever, stray
As long as you think of it this way

Memories of the heart are yours to keep
And when you feel lost, lonely, or even sad
All is needed is to seek
Remember, Love begins within the heart
It was there from the start

12/2003

I Will Always Be Grateful

In Loving Memory
Of Meron Long (My uncle)
Dedicated to his wife, Jane Long

People said that you and I would never make it,
They said I would never be true to you,
And when I made a vow, they said I would break it
They said I wasn't in love with you
Now they know that we are as one,
And I cherish the lovable things you say and do.
With all the love I can give, as long as I live
I'll always be grateful to you

I want the whole wide world to know how much I adore
you.
My heart will follow you where ever you may go,
Time can never erase this love that I have for you,
As the years roll by I love you more and more,
Oh, I know that if I could live my life all over,
I would pray that God would give me you.
Think of the time I could spend, loving you all over again
I would never do anything to make you blue,
But I can't turn back the hands of time,
So I'm going to spend the rest of my life loving you,
With all the love I can give, as long as I live,
I'll always be grateful to you.

Meron Long

Those Sweet Summer Days

In Loving Memory
Of Meron Long (My uncle)
Dedicated to his wife, Jane Long

Those sweet summer days we spent so happily together
   our love was a dream come true
Your eyes seemed to say, that you would love me forever
   as I strolled in the park with you.
June sunshine and flowers
A true love that never strays
Oh I cherish those happy hours
Hurry back sweet summer days

Those sweet summer days, with you on Tahiti Islands
   the cheerful songs of the oriole
With soft evening breezes, and flamingos go flying
   into a beautiful sunset of gold
There in the shadows of the palm trees
Watching the ships and the crashing sea waves
Oh how I long for those happy hours
Hurry back sweet summer days
Those sweet summer days

Meron Long

Encouraging Thoughts

Life is filled with challenges to be accomplished one by one
But, when you feel good about yourself
There's no hurdle you can't overcome!

Annette Whitaker

Who Can I Be

How profound I must be!
Maneuvering cannot be done with me
Timeframes, I have none
Yet, I hold a precious key

To open hearts and minds
Of boys and girls
And all the people of this world
I am found during life's ups and downs
Yet, hidden by an eye that's blind
Destined to change the direction of frowns

For, I can conquer anxiety
Overrule self-denial
Develop hope, with cautiousness
And, I am biased to no society

Wondering now, who can I be?
Be patient, and you will see
Things beginning to unfold
Cause patience is my name, that's
What I'm told

08/23/94

Cherish What's Yours

Cherish what's yours, and it will always belong to
you
Capture the heart of it, so the love will always be
true
Pamper it, nourish it one heart to another
Guard it, so there is no need for others
Appreciate what's yours, and the beauty will show
Reflecting love, care, and honor that will always
glow

01/13/06

Happy Birthday Friend

(Dedicated to Darrell Oliver)

It's an awesome feeling
To meet someone who's willing
To respect another's wishes
When it's not their own issues

Selfishness is not a virtue
It goes against our human nature
But love begins
When selfishness ends
And the heart begins to speak
So the ears begin to hear
What the eyes tend to seek
And the relationship grows more
   and more unique

You are special every day
Even more so today
So feel the love from within
When I say,
Happy Birthday!
To my very special friend

10/26/05

Pity Party Invitation

A pity party, I was invited
A tear dropped from my eye
As I cleared my throat
I began to sigh
Emotionally, screaming "Oh my God, why?"

But my heart said, no my dear, fight against it
You can not go, your faith is too strong to sink this low
Hold your head high and know in your soul
There's a higher power working to achieve a much
better goal

I changed my attitude
For this too shall pass, it will not last
And this much, I did conclude
A pity party, no thanks!
I'm no longer in the mood

For I am more than a conquer!
No matter what life takes me through
God will make a way, today, and every day!
Whether I'm singing a good, bad, or happy song
I will never walk the road alone

So, I RSVP the sender
Hope you are not offended
But, I will not be attending
This pity party is not for me
Cause it's not what God intended!

09/06/05

My Thoughts

I wonder sometimes am I a good judge of character
Purposely, I look for the good in others
I know there is bad in everyone
I want to find that which is good, which brings about a smile,
  peace and joy
Something worthwhile to build upon
My task is to take on challenges
Set examples for all to see
This mission is not impossible
Inner strength is granted to me
Still, I must allow for failures, mistakes, and renewals
Cause lives are as precious jewels

Failure brings about a realization that I can't do it all, nor can I
  do it alone
Though I am bold, and I am strong
My heart, my mind, my soul all goes into it
Reality has its way of letting me know something went wrong
Yet, I can not quit
I must fight, refocus, stay positive, and remain strong

Mistakes, I've made along the way
But, I've learned memorable lessons to always cherish
People say one thing, but do another
Much heartache, I have discovered
But through it all, I did not perish
This is what I share with others
Life has only made me stronger
I can, and I will survive another day longer

Survival depends on what's held inside
Hatred can only grow
Till there's nowhere to reside
Enemies, it will create
Illness may accelerate
Loneliness becomes a friend
Eventually, it reacts
And surroundings begin to end
Life, you once knew
Becomes dark, sad and blue

But, it doesn't have to end that way
A mind is a powerful tool
Change your thinking, and your doing
This is called renewing

04/4/05

Young, Old, and Wise Eyes

Beauty and youth will one day disappear
The aging process soon becomes clear
All are young and foolish
Old, but wise
Having learned and loved through young and old eyes

Laughing, smiling, and holding hands
Playing, dancing, and singing songs
Talking daily, hours at a time
Saying nothing, but I'm glad you're mine
Love is in the air for these young eyes

Weeping, frowning, and agreeing to nothing
Sitting alone, wishing for company
Counting the days as they go by
Wondering what happened and maybe why
Doubt is in the mind of these old eyes

Humbleness, patient, and forgiving
Listening, hearing, and understanding
Being respectful, dependable, truthful and honorable
This is the love of the heart seen through wise eyes

10/29/04

HE

You give him an inch; **he** will take a mile!
You pour your heart out to him; **he** will try and catch it!
You tell him that you have someone but timing is all
wrong,
He will work that much harder to set things right, to put it
in place, to sing your song!
He isn't that crazy to not know; vulnerability is the time to
show!
He, a man willing to go over and beyond
As **he** competes, while showing you a little fun
Once upon a time, **he** was the one!
And now, that time is over and done!
He, who once, had no interest in my heart,
Today, said **he** wants a new start
I will never forget how **he**, befriended me!
Now, friendship is all I want it to be!

12/03/04

Who Am I To Judge

The mind changes from day to day
Attitude portrays the good you see
What I offer you, I offer no other
Yet, I claim all as my sisters, my brothers

I listen to your every word
Your love, your heartbreak
Your pain, your sorrows
Then, wonder what mistake you'll make tomorrow

I wish you the best in all you do
But sneer like the rest when your best pull through
Jealousy consumes me, and I can't get free
Cause what you have, I want for me

But, I love you, I really do!
The best is all I want for you
This madness is no isolated case
Its there, hidden behind the smiles of every face

Then I lift my eyes above wondering, Lord, how is this love
With a comforting sigh
Suddenly, I realize why
This type of love had to die

I am just a human being
By no means, am I perfect
Though, I have qualities for forgiveness and love
I am not qualified, at all, to judge!

12/01/04

I AM Blessed

Tender years
Filled with love and laughter
The teaching of pioneers
Strong morals forever after
Mother, with a spouse
Siblings to arouse
Hurdles to cross
A home, not a house
Who would ask for less?
Thank You, Lord
For, I am blessed

With a high tolerance for undesired circumstances
Pains of the heart are scattered and confused
Desperately seeking direction
There are so many choices to choose
But only one within my heart
Lord, it's your word I choose to use
Who would ask for less?
Thank You, Lord
For, I am blessed

Conscious of one's own identity
Wanting to be seen, heard, praised and loved
Struck by deceit, yet unheard of
Lost for a moment
Still, strength was granted
Will, was planted
No pity, no doubt, no shame
See, these things, I overcame

Who would ask for less?
Thank You, Lord
For, I am blessed

Doors of opportunity granted to me
Drawing releases feelings that words cannot
express
Painting conveys the mood and its swift change
Writing connects words to express meaningful
ideas
These are talents that show my best
All with a personality of perseverance
Who would ask for less?
Thank You, Lord
For, I am blessed

10/20/04

3D Signs

Mentioned several times
Not looking for a hit and run relationship
Need a handyman who loves, not love then leave
But, you <u>did</u>

Friends, you say
That means someone on the side
Is it or not?
Talk about it; you <u>didn't</u>
But, there's nothing we shouldn't talk about

Wrote a letter
To kiss and make up
Is that what friends do?
They do but <u>don't</u>

Leave, you <u>did</u>
Talk, you <u>didn't</u>
Makeup, you <u>don't</u>

<u>Did</u>, <u>Didn't</u>, and <u>Don't</u>
The 3D signs
What kind of love is this?
Truly, not a good kind!

07/20/04

Companionship

I said I need a handyman
Someone to mend my broken heart
To fix my broken pipes
To help me in the yard
Travel with me to see the sights
On a plane or a ship
I said I need companionship!

Someone to wash my car
To fix my breaks
To protect my name, my heart, my soul
I need someone I can appreciate
To cook and clean
And wash the clothes
Someone to share the household work
And expenses, I should mention
I need a handyman with good intentions

I said I need a handyman
First a friend, a husband, a lover
To extend a woman's nature
To flirt, to cuddle and discover
Happiness as it uncovers
Passions of a relationship
I said I need companionship!

07/12/04

Attachment

As friends, we are open and honest
With laughter and enjoyment of the company
  of one another
Still, somehow we close the doors hiding the feelings

 we have for the other
While precious moments so swiftly pass away
Foolishly, we continue to say
Or ask ourselves is that what friends do each and
  every day?
Very cautious, not to cross the lines
Ensuring the friendship is never dying

But the friendship, we will always cherish
Whatever the situation, hopefully, it will never perish
For friends, it begins
And as friends, it shall never end

Though, I have no claims
The attachment to you is strong
My heart for you, I aim
Uncertain if this is where it belongs
Still, inside I hope you feel the same

Yet, I wonder, the attachment is it wrong?
And slowly I redirect my feelings, cares, and thoughts
Respectfully, putting them where they ought
And the desires that wander deep inside
Gradually, dissipate where loneliness resides

And I realize an attachment is just that
Removable where unwanted
Replaceable with security, allowing happiness to
mature
Attaching hearts so love can endure

07/06/04

My Tears

Tears of despair
Invades my heart
I am speechless
Surrounded with air that I can not breathe
Slowly, a small grasp of oxygen enters my lungs
Barely, understanding that I must go on

Pull it together, I say
Piece by piece
Battle this stormy weather
Acknowledge this grief
The pain shall pass
Though not forgotten
Sight beyond the tears, at last, I've gotten

But, how do I love anyone else?
Never have I been by myself
There is no song if you are gone
Yet, my tears say to me
Baby, keep pushing on

05/18/04

We Witness

We go through something
We Survive
We live through something
We rise
Then, we witness

Our heart breaks
We weaken
We recover
Our spirit strengthen
Then, we witness

We Struggle
But overcome
We believe
Hope it becomes
Then, we witness

We live, we learn
We help, we care
We give, we love
We share, we witness!

01/18/04

Realistic Aid

To be genuine is to offer realistic aid
A guarantee that will not fade
But the truth is yet to be accepted
And, deceit becomes more adapted

In time of need
What shall we seek?
In our minds, it's money, we think
When loneliness takes its peak
Companionship we hope to meet

When there's sadness,
That we cannot comprehend
Giving up becomes a friend
Determination meets its end
And living, well it depends!

Good intentions, it's understood
But, the aid, it's no good
Realistically, what we seek
Is love our heart and soul to keep

There's no comfort like that above
Realistic aid, undying love
His word has never fade
His help, he always engages

For he is the truth that cannot be hidden
And he is the light that's never forbidden
Trust him and see for yourself
His love is like no one else

10/21/02

Reaching Out

When the doors are closed
And the heart is at a lost
Speaking of love
But know not how

Acknowledging pain
The feeling of hatred
That doesn't let go of love
But battles selfishness
And the belief to just hold on

Not blind to what it sees or believes
But have lost directions
And have no connections
Only hope for someone to intervene

But the doors are closed
And many steps are needed to open it
Just don't give up
Reach out in prayer, faith, and love

08/18/02

How Should We Live

Unspoken words piercing the heart
Speechless, disappointment from the very start
When will we understand?
In order to live
We must take a stand

Give love; it comes from the heart
Consideration and appreciation
Fills our life with great expectations
It's part of the plan
As our lives began to expand

Give obedience, to self and others
Paving the way for patient and endurance
Teaching to strive further and further
Guaranteeing, with faith, full assurance
Ourselves shall we discover

Give guidance, to develop confidence
Unspoken words, we shall hear
Encourage trustworthiness, speechlessness
dissolves
Love, Obedience, Guidance we give
And it becomes evidence of how we lived

08/07/02

Hopes For Tomorrow

Our skin may be different
And so may our hair
But we all have one heart
And our creator
Yes, he put it there

We strive hard
For the opportunity to compete
Not to prove who's strong
Or who's weak
But to guarantee our children
Our lives can be sweet
To set examples, goals, and desires
That someday our children
They too will be hired

They too will be promoted
Instead of low raises
For being so devoted
And accumulating praises

This is a message
Hear it! Loud and Clear
Feel the essence
For the future is near

Dreams that come true
Are hopes for tomorrow
For you and for me
An end to our sorrows

06/09/02

Mr. Massey

Almost a year
Acquainted with only your voice
The thought of you makes me cheer
And wonder the other choice

Tall, handsome, low profile
Excellent mannerism is what I envision
A man of many words
Mysteriously spoken
Quiet, but not shy
Full of precision
Will another year pass me by?

Chasing a man is not my style
But, my imagination is running wild
If, nothing else.....
Returning a favor is what I wish
A simple smile will comes out of this!

P.S.

Now is not the time
To send you a Valentine
But a few kind rhymes
May, someday, make you mine
Therefore, I say
To Mr. Massey anyway
Happy Valentine's Day!

02/10/2001

I Am

I am filled with life
Able to feel joy
Able to express pain
Words display deceit
That only I can explain

Bitterness can overwhelm me
Humbleness can restore me
Chaos pierces
But, love replenishes

Created by our father above
When life ends
It is I, who will be judged
For, I am smart
Because I am heart!

09/22/00

Massage

Massage me!
Mind, body, and soul
Let my heart run free
As emotions take its toll

Touch the spot that's deeply stressed
Release the joys that lie at rest
Relaxation, I'll find while on this quest
Exploring the mind without regrets

Massage me!
Noon till night
Mind, body, and soul
Experiencing an unforgettable flight

09/17/2000

A Personal Prayer

Lord, I ask for a man that I can be proud of being loved by,
  as you would have a husband love his wife

Please put someone in my path who respects me, not envy me
Someone who will protect me with his love for you,
  not someone who will deceitfully try to destroy my spirits,
  or my glow of self-determination

Let that special someone keep me on the narrow and straight
  path of righteousness
Not someone who tries to confuse your word or use your word
  to conquer self-desires

Please send someone I can talk with about anything, and in that
  everything I say or do is held in confidence
So, when I cry he will know it's not time to laugh, but time to
  comfort
And when there are moments of laughter, they are to be shared,
  not divided, not despised

For you know the plans you have for me
Plans to prosper and not harm me
Plans to give me hope and a future
Your plans are better than I can ever image or hope for
Lord, this time, I want things to be different with all of your
  blessings
I ask for a man that I can be proud of being loved by,
  as you would have a husband love his wife

Amen

Sadden Hearts

Too many years of our life spent together
Not all of it was bliss
Our love, I thought, would last forever
And most of it, I'll miss
Never in my wildest dreams
Did I know it would end with such a scheme
I never knew how sadden hearts
Would someday keep our love apart

I always felt that you would leave
This my sadden heart truly believed
Though high hopes that things would change
To everlasting happiness and love we gain
I never knew our sadden hearts
Would someday keep our love apart

Cripple and denture wearing
I thought we would be
Sitting together holding our young ones
One on each knee
Telling tales of how we were
How no one believed it would ever occur
I never knew our sadden hearts
Would someday keep our love apart

Conquered all, I thought we had done
But sadden hearts has stolen our fun
Life, as I had hoped, has yet to begin
With many clouds
And very little sun
I never knew our sadden hearts
Would someday keep our love apart

11/23/99

~ 30 ~

Young Eyes

The promise of chortle found in young eyes
Willful heart not hardened with pride
They are precious with the gesture of a dove
Strengthened by the father's love

11/19/99

Destiny

It was said to me
"You can't."
But, I could
I did
I would
And I will again

Dreaming is whatever
I want it to be
Ending hopelessly with can't
Or continuing endlessly with can
My destiny is mines
Because I believe I can

It was said to me
"You can't."
But, I could
I did
I would
And I will again

02/10/97

Peace Makers

Please, to all of you who are at war
Ease the pain that brings not happiness, but
  disaster for many near and far
Adversity is here; it's there, wherever
  we are
Cease the blood shed falsely done
  proclaiming to restore

Who are the peacemakers?
You, me, and our neighbors next door
Demand unity, be stronger than ever before
Unite our worlds, to preserve and to adore
For anything less, will only destroy

06/06/96

Something You Say

Self-esteem is needed
But, for some, it's not easy to achieve
It's part of what is believed
  nurtured by those who guide, not misleads

Should you say something motivational
To brighten someone's day or
Should you say something heartbreaking
  to blow their mind away
Should you say something encouraging
True or false, with no consideration of the
  cost or
Should you say something wrong or right
With possible cause for defense or maybe
  a fight

Please be careful of what you say
Complementing creates a reason to strive
Criticizing tends only to viciously drive
Don't take life away
Simply, because of something you say

02/27/96

Some Days

Some Days I just don't know
  what I'm doing wrong
At night, I can't sleep
By morning, my spirits are high
Mid-day, I think my saga is ended
But come evening, I'm singing
  that same ole song
Oh, Lord, what is it that I've
  done wrong

I start with the feeling everything
  will soon be alright
Knowing faith comes without a trace
  of sight
My spirits are high and I'm walking
  on air
But with a bat of an eye, I'm feeling
  low with no hopes or belief to spare
Singing that same ole song
Oh, Lord, what is it that I've
    done wrong

11/27/95

Where I Started

Right back where I started
Am I any smarter
Maybe
Any richer
Any happier
No

Have I lost faith
Given up
Become hopeless
Or feeble
No

Still
Strong will
More determine
Self-confident
Yes, right back where I started

12/19/95

Waiting To Be Found

Love is all around
With a sweet soft voice
And many gentle hugs
Feeling and needing a touch of
   smooth skin
And countless ways of saying, love

Writing seen in beautiful eyes
And tears that read I need you
There's a sense of closeness shared
Knowing each day brings a new

But sometimes it's lost or hidden
And one needs to stop and listen
Love has a wonderful sound
It resides deep inside
Just waiting somewhere to be found

12/13/95

We Have Dreams Too

We are the ones with a dream
That our lives will become easier
To see sunshine most days
And many pleasant nights
The dream is not to be rich
But comfortable, content, and happy
Knowing in our hearts
It will pass from this generation
   and generations thereafter

For we see other's dreams come true
And inside we are bitter
Happy we really are for those most
   fortunate
Worthy or not, we try not to judge
But a thought from us who are weary
Please give us just a little
It will carry us a long way
Giving us confidence and strength every day
Those who have, have dreams
But we who don't have dreams too

12/10/95

Look At Me

Look at me
What do you see?
One of beauty
Filled with self-esteem
One with nothing
But, capable of everything
Look at me, but judge me not
Use the shoes that I have used
Then you will know, its hope
I choose

Look at me
What do you see?
Rejoicing or agony
Holding my head high
Walking each day at a time
Worrying is a festival heavily
  on my mind
But, with a clear conscience, my
  Thoughts remain the same
Everything is possible, this I
  Have ordained
Look at me, but judge me not
Use the shoes that I have used
Then you will know, its hope
I choose

It's hope I choose to see me
  through
With hope, I know I can not lose
Look at me, but judge me not
Use the shoes that I have used
Then you will know, its hope
I choose

11/20/95

Days To Cherish

New and old beginnings
Sweethearts on Valentine
Four-leaf-cover, a symbol of
    good luck
Love or con on April Fool
Forget-me-not, on Mother's Day
Love you Pop, on Father's Day
Sparkles of joy, for Independent
    we are
Full moon, let our secrets out
Lazy Daisies on Labor Day
Dares to seem on Halloween
Still together for Thanksgiving
Sharing and planning for Christmas Eve
Christmas Day, the year is ending
January 1st, a new beginning

But days to cherish are always seen
And other days are far and between
Artificial, they are not
Just days to cherish of the week
Are days to cherish and days to keep

When a mouth can't speak
But, an ear can hear
And, an eye can see
When the mind is weak
And thoughts are few
And ideas seem lost, these are signs
  of becoming meek

But a helping hand is always there
Guiding us through another day
Bringing smiles every way
Helping to reach a higher peak
Remember, every day of the week
Are days to cherish and days to keep

03/02/95

Your Spirit

(Dedicated To Rebecca McBride)
"Big Mama"

You visited me late one night
Shortly after you passed
I tossed and turned trying to fight
Cause you're present, I could not grasp

Though, I saw nothing
But the imprint as you sat
My heart, felt something
Your spirit, I'll never forget

Frightened, I could not reach out
My eyes, I closed, then you left
Afraid to shout
Because I knew I was there by myself

But, was it to say one last goodbye
Or to check on me, as you often did
Maybe to say, I'm going to heaven now,
   don't you cry
Be good, dear, my sweet little kid

You were with me, and will always be
Your spirit is in my heart
Your warmth comes to my memory
That love will never part

And though you visited me, I saw
   nothing
But the imprint as you sat
My heart, felt something
Your spirit, Lord knows, I'll never forget

10/13/94

Send Me One Good Man

I ask you
Lord, if you can
Send me one good man
Me, I want him to understand

Let him feel my pain
And I the same
Let us omit the childish games
Unity Lord, I pray we gain

Let him have a kind heart
Even, let his mind be smart
This way Lord, he will always know
Never, ever, will we part

Selfish, I know this may sound
Still, let him play on my playground
All the others, they will frown
But remember Lord, he's my crown

Let him, Lord, laugh and play
Express his love in many ways
Make us special on holidays
Keep us together every day

Let him admire only me
So, I and the world will see
This man, Lord,
You sent to me

And most of all
Let him love you
Like so few of them do
Let him fear you, Lord
So our life can be new

I ask you
Lord, if you can
Send me one good man

09/04/94

True Success

Prosperity feeds on envy
While corrupting a willing mind
It deteriorates the body
And affects all of mankind

Its belief of success
Dress with a smile
But elegant material values
Are everything but worthwhile

True happiness we seek
But never seem to find
A never-ending chase
To feel more and more divine

Believe and acknowledge
He who created night and day
With one single word
Can bring happiness your way

Let it be known
With your heart, seek his pleasures
True success can be rewarding
As well as unmeasured

07/26/94

How Can I

How can I keep this secret to myself
Knowing all alone there's someone else
How can I smile with tears traveling
   from mile to mile
Knowing my heart is in constant denial

How can I tell him, my friend, he is
That my man has a thing for that girl
   of his
How can I keep myself in between
This love, the friendship, this
   disgusting thing

How can I explain, knowing things are
   not the same
How can I erase this pain
So that I may truly love again

How can I keep him to myself
And expose him to no one else
How can I believe he's mine, all mine
When his feelings are so undefined

How can I regain the love I've lost
Bring him back forever more
At what price will cost
To release the love that I have stored

06/25/94

Best Friend

(Dedicated to Andrea Lightfoot)

With love comes pain and joy
That cannot be escaped by anyone
Guidance is given to us all
Old, young, big, or small
Even babies who can not crawl

When it's time to turn away
God, for sure, will not astray
Life is designed for all mankind
So that we may truly find
Deep inside a peace of mind

Warmth arrives from within
In knowing you have one best friend
Without creating any demands
To listen and understand
If you decide to amend your plans

To turn a frown into a smile
Help forget the pain for a while
To share the joy
We gladly employ
That is what true friends are for

Receiving that special care
You just can't find anywhere
Originality is the blend
Which is where you fit in portraying the
  Role of my best friend

5/4/94

Encouragement

(Dedicated to Sharon Rueter)

Enlighten with all that was good
Reap the joy only some understood
Negligence, you know, played no part
In aiding a sad and broken heart
Captured by your love and concern
Friendship, then, you were able to earn
Open-minded was how it began
A strong foundation was what you formed

Uttered the sweetest words
Only my ears could have heard
The reality, I was forced to see
And your guidance was there for me
Abandoned me, you never did
Only pampered me, just like a kid
Generosity, you extended to me
Gave your service without a fee

Excellence was what you taught
Even when I badly fought
Meaningful you're always been
In our hearts, we were always kin
Encouragement was what you gave
Never knowing how much you saved
Nourishing a friend in need
Surpasses all the friendly deeds
Thinking of you brought a smile
Those lessons in life were surely worthwhile

04/28/94

A Woman's Love

With a heart of assurance
Full of faith and endurance
Deeper than the eyes can see
A woman's love is eternity

Though, she is often faced
   with dissent
And frustrations diverge
Her love, she always presents
And her faith is always
   Encouraged

Even, when love seems hopeless
Her heart can still be read
Her mind is still in focus
Only seeking to be fed

And like a thief in the night
Words are unspoken
He comes as expected
And her arms are wide open

As the heat surpasses
The mind is taken on an
   angel's flight
The hopelessness disappears
   fast
During that special moment
   of delight

But, that feeling goes
Again, he annihilates her
   heart
Leaving her many woes
Still, she smiles and raises
   Her eyes to the stars

Other wonders, why
Her heart and this reality
She responds without being shy
And with great dignity

Because her heart is filled
   with assurance
Along with faith and endurance
Her love grows deeper than the
   eyes can see
A woman's love is eternity

03/10/94

Thank You, Lord

Though we try hard to live a good life
Being extra careful to obey your commandments
The struggle gets harder
Traveling through a path that isn't very nice

And punished we sometimes feel
For reasons certainly unseen
Cause of the life we live
Retaliate we'll never dream

But, we know
Your eyes aren't blind to such a sight
We believe in you, Lord
To reap a heart filled with delight

For you, Oh Lord
Have been our salvation
You heard our cries
And you carried us through
Our tears were dried
And our lives restored as new
For this, Oh Lord, we thank you!

11/05/93

Deep In Heart

Excluded me from your talks
Yet, I'm constantly in your thoughts
Confide in someone dear
And tell me there's no fear
Still, deep in heart
You are here

Welcoming with open arms
Persuading with all your charms
Tell me I'm your special mate
Deceive me on a date
Still, deep in heart
I can not escape

Maybe there's no cheating
But, why is my heart bleeding
Your eyes are always blind
But, to others they are fine
Still, deep in heart
I know you are mine

Run, Run, Runaway
True love can never astray
But, if or when you leave someday
Deep in heart
You will always stay

10/26/93

A Cry For Peace

How is it that we know one another so
 well
Yet, life together is simply hell
Clearly, we can see the pain
Knowing this love is no game

Love grows deeper than eyes can see
With such a submissive personality
But will you ever just understand me
And know how I want this love to be

There's not a huge difference between
 you and I
Concerns lie with the question why
What we perceive seems to deceive
Making it easy for confusion to conceive

Feeling the wind as we pass
Trying hard not to crash
Releasing that disguising sigh
Lonely hearts begin to cry

A cry for peace
For agreement has ceased
A cry for love
Reaching high above

10/20/93

Dedicated To Nin Kent

Nurtured us all with your heart of gold
Innocent love, you were able to unfold
Needed you were for the world to see
The aim in life is what we wanted it to be

Kneel forever with a mind at ease
Everlasting love, you are sure to receive
Notable deeds you left behind
Tenderness now is sure to shine

We shared the bliss that you extended
Special to us you will always be
Part of this happy family
Hoping someday that we will see
You again, eternally
But, until that wonderful and embellished day
In our hearts DEAR, you will always stay

08/25/93

World Of Mystery

Escape into this mystery
Where evil has no place
Bliss is overwhelming
And there are no obstacles to face
Invade the world of fantasy
Enjoy the make believe
Reality has no destiny
And character has no need

Glide towards a diverse century
Where birds are standing tall
With children, they are playing
Singing pass to me, pass to all

Everyone is laughing
Carefree love is grasping
Melodies are flowing
Creeping near and far
To all living creatures
Longing to hear more

Possessed by its beauty
Images one can see
Cruising along an amazing sky
Relaxing the mind and setting it free
Glaze into this world so high
Encounter the smile of secrecy
Filled in a world of mystery

08/25/93

When Things Are Blue

When things are blue
Turn to the Lord
For only he will comfort you

When no one seems to care
And your heart is saddened
When life just seems unfair
Talk to him
And you will find
These things you can share

There is nothing new
His ears haven't heard
Nothing impossible
He can't accomplish
Trust in him
His word is true
Be assured
He is there for you

Amazed you will be
When the burden is lifted
And your mind is free
To enjoy life as our Lord
meant it to be

08/10/93

A Beautiful Person

Beholds the essence of her love

Extends the quality of her warmth

Admires the beauty that she possesses

Upholds righteousness for her success

Teaches the splendor of her love

Impresses with her caring heart

Fascinates and glorifies for what she
  believes in

Utilizes the good in all she sees

Learns from what she perceives

Progresses through wisdom

Enamors those who hate

Ridicules no one for heaven's sake

Speculates on happy deeds

Offers kindness to those in need

Nurtures the body, heart, and soul
  to succeed

06/30/93

Lost Friendship

(Dedicated to a childhood friend)

In a world filled with unpredictable
  circumstances
And destiny, as we know it
Conquers our desires
Friendship becomes Paradox of Hedonism
Opening doors for much criticism

When all these things are vivid
Friendship is forgiving
Understanding one another
Accepting things that can not be changed
Realizing fault may not have been intentional
Friendship, like love, is unconditional

Friends, though different
Communication must exist
Laugh and sometimes cry
Even, play a stubborn role
Or, let our pride be the guide
But, friendship should be as solid as gold

Remember as the years may pass
Someday, by faith, we may unite
Reminisce and replenish that special love
Planted deep inside us from above

05/21/93

What They Told Me

They told me to go to school
Get an education
End the field work
Passed from generation to generation

They told me of the physical and mental
  pain
To work so hard
To be whipped, burned, or hanged
All for such little gain
Called the success of a black man

I went to school
Got an education
The field work may have changed
But, not the physical and mental pain

I work in an office atmosphere
Where it is cool in the summer
And warm in the winter
Comfortable, one might say
But, equal, it is not

Though, I do the same work
 My reward is not the same pay
Though, I work the same hours
My recognition is diminished every day
Though, I smile and get along with others
My attitude needs adjusting, they say
Though, I have the same understanding
  and I.Q.

Endlessly, I am forced to mention that

famous word, "sue."

One excuse behind another
To keep me constantly struggling
In memory of my black brothers
The vivid control over me and others

They told me to go to school
Get an education
And end the field work
Passed from generation to generation
Did they forget to tell me
Or, did they not know
Success in the business world is not
    determined by how good I may be
But, that their acceptance is the key

Maybe, I did not comprehend
That education is where it begins
And deployment without ammunition
Is only invaluable intuition
Now, I can clearly see
The importance of what they told me

04/03/93

Misconceptions

The media focuses heavily on robberies, drugs, and
killings
While portraying black society as the villains
How can we be so simple-minded to believe blacks are
    the only participants
And yet, we all are suffering drastically by the millions

Turn to a talk show during working hours
Or pick up a newsstand magazine
Who do you find stealing the precious dollar
Bank fraud, the prestigious white collar

Who would kill a family member to collect on
    insurance claim
Then premeditate the alleged killer
Just to clear his name
Not the poor black society who can't afford the fame

Who supports the psychologists
To rehabilitate their young
Drug addicts, alcoholics, runaways, and prostitution
Surely, not that disgusting sight
Television has managed to show with such delight

And who abuse their parents
Or send them to an old folk's home
Cause life is just too short
To pamper, love, or care
For an old feeble body
No longer able to roam

A deliberate misconception
Is all it seems to be
From the authority of the media's nominees
Beware of such illusions
And the harm that it creates
By its discriminating conclusions
Society is who it forsakes

01/28/93

A Child's Perspective

How long must we endure the agony
of the world
Which seems to be filled with such
heartless people
Ignorant to the fact that harshness,
unfairness and greediness cause hatred
But a kind word or deed reveals the joy
and freedom of living

Remembering as a child who knew nothing
of money
How a kiss would cause the disappearance
of pain
And a simple, but special touch would
create a giggle
Or how a restless night came to its end
When the words good night and I Love
You were whispered
And the importance of life, as a child,
was a family united happily together

For loneliness had no meaning
To the heart of a child
Love was always screening
Rejoicing and running wild

Filled with anticipation
The sound of jiggling keys
Expression of fascination
Was wonderful to receive

A pure heart could not resist the charm
So sweet and innocent
Running toward one with open arms
Eagerly awaiting true complement

Fulfilled, a child must certainly be
If people of the world could only see
Gathering around in harmony
Love is all we really need

Surely, if people of the world could see
from a child's perspective
How the words coupled with a kiss and
a touch
Converts into bliss

Then, maybe the endurance of all agony
would end
And we all may live in unity
Thus, eliminating sin

01/20/93

The Power of Faith

The unknown can be disturbing
Causing anxiety and frustrations
Soon impatience creeps along
And the imagination begins to rome

Options seem few
Solutions, impossible
Determination slowly deteriorates
And, hope is interrogated

But, Faith, a powerful tool
Awaits you
It reveals no evidence
Yet, required complete confidence

For the Power of Faith
Removes obstacles
Retains relaxation
And righteousness, as it deserves
Is rewarded for holding true
To the one and only faith

Because God was acknowledged
When all seemed blue
That optimistic attitude
Will always comfort you

12/8/92

Deceitful Eyes

The innocent soul
Unaware of what life will unfold
The struggles of success
Hidden behind closed doors
From those deceitful eyes
But, friendly smiles
Yet, mischievously awaiting to scorn
Another goal of the innocent soul

Ironically,
Rules and requirements change
But, lauded again for the achievement
Of most tolerant
Despite the many obstacles
That lie before
The innocent soul with a heart of gold

Still, contemplating defeat
Sadness is revealed
For the inner peace
Warmth for others
Contentment
Faith and patient
Deceitful eyes can see
But, cannot understand
The hearts of the innocent soul

As they lobby on such illusions
A positive effect is their conclusion
But in the end, that dreadful end
A second chance they would gladly mend
Had they known what the innocent souls
  have always shown

09/30/92

Mind of All Minds

Creating many wonders
Enchanting rainbows
Uproarious thunder
Shining stars delighted with moonlight
And the surrounding chasms

Mind of all minds
And its glorious creations
Have eyes of magnificence that lie upon all

The buds to roses
The caterpillars to butterflies
The fetus to human
The cyclones to hurricanes
And season to season

Mind of all minds
And its glorious creations
Have eyes of magnificence that lie upon all

Through all its wonders
Teaches the art of patience
While enduring the frustrations
Of denied expectations
The pains of love
And meaningless confrontations

Mind of all minds
And its glorious creations
Have eyes of magnificence that lie upon all

Debut of life
A complicated rotation
Filled with dissonance
Elated with hope

Mind of all minds
And its glorious creations
Have eyes of magnificence that lie upon all

8/26/92

Love Me

Love me for who I am
Or maybe someday
Share with me daily trials
  and tribulations in every way

Respect my views
Complicated, wrong, or right
Do not despair
Exhibit your compassion
Declare love that we must share

Love me freely
Compatible or not
Explore me
Feel the desire awaiting release
Fulfill all my empty spots

Unconditional love
That is the key
To be successful
In loving me

7/31/92

Impoverish Hearts

People of the world
Wandering amiss
Suppressed by one another
Filled with such inanities
Impoverished hearts
Afraid to love
Only hope is God Above

Politicians with their digression
Exonerating themselves
Proclaiming no differentiating
But deployed we are
Accomplishing nothing
Descending rapidly
Becoming more raucous
Impoverished hearts
Afraid to love
Only hope is God Above

Embellished world
Enormously designed
For all its people, every kind
In unity, we can dissipate the hatred
Enjoy the affluence of its creation
Impoverished hearts
Afraid to love
Only hope is God Above

A world freely given
With a few stipulations
Love and Obedience
We should be thankful
Impoverished hearts
Afraid to love
Only hope is God Above

7/22/92

Yours Forever

Babies, like enchanted toys
Accountable for many joys
Belonging close to the heart
Yours forever, they never part

Expression of love
With one single hug
Innocent souls
Awaiting to fold

Releases a tear
And somewhere near
Baby knows
Affection shows

Laugh so pretty
Technique so witty
Mind so inquisitive
Still so sensitive

Develops identity
Through life's infinity
Still needs caressing
Uplifting and expressing

Babies, like enchanted toys
Accountable for many joys
Belonging close to the heart
Yours forever, they never part

06/09/92

In This Dirty World of Ours

With no respect for others
Each of us turns our heads further
People are killing people
Prices are setting us deeper
We can't sleep
We can't eat
We have nothing to give
We have nothing to keep
Oh! These hard times
Doesn't fulfill this heart of mine

Solution to problems
Our loved ones say
Drugs are the answer
Drugs are the way

Now that we have polluted the world
Are we satisfied with our condition?
Is it safe to walk out the door?
Without hope of living forever more
Barely surviving hour by hour
In this dirty world of ours

10/28/07

To My Husband

Now, when I think of you
Oh! How my face starts glowing
You fill my heart with joy
And now, the love is flowing

In you, I see
How love is supposed to be
And all my thanks
I know, I owe to thee

To have a man like you
It is every girl's dream come true
It shows in everything you do
Your sweet, gentle kiss
Your tender hug
Your kind words
The way you handle situations
Proves, Honey, you're a dove

Your loveable ways
As a lover, a friend
Darling, I will cherish until the end

Your delightful ways
As a husband, a father
Sweetheart, it shows every day
In your son, wife, and daughter
The only tears left to fall
Are happy ones
Maybe none at all
For, we have truly won
So let me take this time to say
Baby, Happy Anniversary Day!

Mother and Child

You search for a name
One that doesn't quite
    sound the same
As the pain comes fast
You hope for the last
To see a boy or a girl
Then, to show the world

Once either is here
No more fear
So much love to offer
Wanting them never to suffer

You watch the wonderful smiles
Emotions so mild
They cuddle and roll
As they grow and grow
Suddenly, they're old
Expecting children of their own

You are now reminiscing
Of life's discovery
As parents yourself
Your hearts are uniting
Both mother and child
Surely, a moment worthwhile!

Gossiping Women

Sitting around the table
Gossiping as most women do
Unlike some who aren't able
They tell everything they know
About the Joneses
What their neighbor owns
Who is right or wrong
Even, what is heard over the phone

Worst of all
Women who gossip usually have more
   problems than anyone else
Their biggest problem
They can't solve them by themselves
So they sit and talk
With ears wide open
Just to tell what is spoken

11/6/82

A Hard Working Man

For the care of his children and his wife
He pays the bills
Helps when ill
Gives that special sample
Of setting a good example

He shows his family the love, happiness, and care
While assuring them, he will always be there
Confident to get the job done
He is a fighting man
Whose fight is never won!

11/06/82

www.ingramcontent.com/pod-product-compliance
Lightning Source LLC
Chambersburg PA
CBHW031604040426
42452CB00006B/407